An Insider's Guide to
BASKETBALL

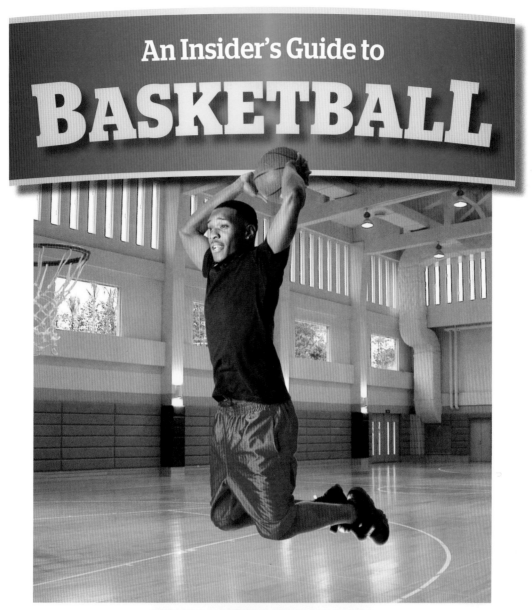

FOREST G. CAMPBELL AND FRED RAMEN

rosen publishing's
rosen
central

NEW YORK

Published in 2015 by The Rosen Publishing Group, Inc.
29 East 21st Street, New York, NY 10010

First Edition

Library of Congress Cataloging-in-Publication Data

Campbell, Forest G.
An insider's guide to basketball/by Forest G. Campbell and Fred Ramen.
    p. cm.—(Sports tips, techniques, and strategies)
Includes bibliographic references and index.
ISBN 978-1-4777-8581-2 (library binding)—ISBN 978-1-4777-8582-9 (pbk.)—
ISBN 978-1-4777-8584-3 (6-pack)
1. Basketball—Juvenile literature. 2. Basketball—Training—Juvenile literature. I. Campbell, Forest G. II. Title.
GV885.1 C36 2015
796.323—d23

Manufactured in Malaysia

Metric Conversion Chart			
1 inch	2.54 centimeters 25.4 millimeters	1 cup	250 milliliters
1 foot	30.48 centimeters	1 ounce	28 grams
1 yard	.914 meters	1 fluid ounce	30 milliliters
1 square foot	.093 square meters	1 teaspoon	5 milliliters
1 square mile	2.59 square kilometers	1 tablespoon	15 milliliters
1 ton	.907 metric tons	1 quart	.946 liters
1 pound	454 grams	355 degrees F	180 degrees C
1 mile	1.609 kilometers		

Contents

CHAPTER 1

Basketball: A History

Basketball, in every sense, is a completely American sport, yet one that enjoys international interest. Unlike many other major sports, basketball did not evolve from other games or have an origin shrouded in myths and legends. It was invented by a single person in 1891, and since then has become popular throughout the world.

Tony Parker of France, among the world's best players, plays for the NBA.

People of both sexes and of all ages play pick-up games in back yards, at gyms, and at playgrounds around the globe. College and university teams vie for championships every year. In addition, countries in North and South America, Europe, Asia, Africa, and Australia have their own professional men's leagues. Some of the best players from around the world now play in North America's National Basketball Association (NBA), including Tony Parker of France and Yao Ming of China.

Basketball's popularity is easy to understand. In the first place, it doesn't require a lot of equipment—just a hoop, a ball, and a flat, hard surface. Besides, anyone can play the sport, because it emphasizes agility and conditioning over physical strength. You don't even have to be tall: Muggsy Bogues, who played for several NBA teams in the 1980s and 1990s, stood 5 feet 3 inches.

Basketball is a fun activity for you and your friends, and it's also a great way to improve your conditioning and coordination. So, it's no surprise that so many people play this great American game.

James Naismith: The Inventor of Basketball

Basketball was invented in America and first played by Americans, but the sport had an international flavor from the beginning. That's because the man who invented it was Canadian.

In 1891, James Naismith was a young teacher at the YMCA Training School in Springfield, Massachusetts. The school's physical education department wanted to develop a game that would be fun to play indoors, when the snow and cold made it impossible to send the young men outside. Naismith wanted to create

A statue of Dr. James Naismith, the inventor of basketball, is located on a plaza at Springfield College in Springfield, Massachusetts.

an indoor version of soccer or football, but was afraid that it would be too rough for a confined space. Instead, he invented his own game, developing thirteen simple rules for play. Players had to shoot a large ball into a basket that was located high off the floor. They were not allowed to tackle or interfere with the person who held the ball, and could not run with the ball.

The Thirteen Original Basketball Rules

Here are James Naismith's original basketball rules. According to legend, he came up with the rules in about an hour. Most of them are still in effect in modified form today:

1. The ball may be thrown in any direction with one or both hands.

2. The ball may be batted in any direction with one or both hands.

3. A player cannot run with the ball. The player must throw it from the spot on which he catches it, allowances to be made for a man who catches the ball when running if he tries to stop.

4. The ball must be held by the hands. The arms or body must not be used for holding it.

5. No shouldering, holding, pushing, tripping, or striking in any way the person of an opponent shall be allowed; the first infringement of this rule by any player shall come as a foul, the second shall disqualify him until the next goal is made, or, if there was evident intent to injure the person, for the whole of the game, no substitute allowed.

6. A foul is striking the ball with the fist, violation of Rules 3, 4, and such as described in Rule 5.

7. If either side makes three consecutive fouls it shall count as a goal for the opponents (consecutive means without the opponents in the meantime making a foul).

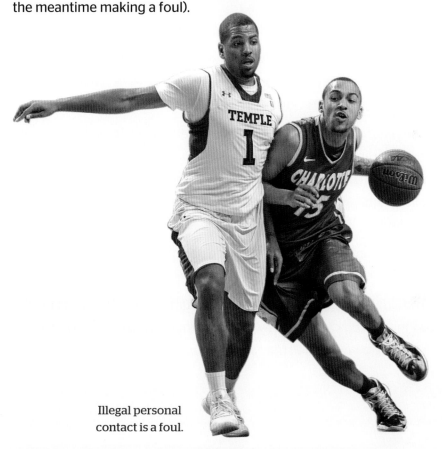

Illegal personal contact is a foul.

8. A goal shall be made when the ball is thrown or batted from the grounds into the basket and stays there, providing those defending the goal do no touch or disturb the goal. If the ball rests on the edges, and the opponent moves the basket, it shall count as a goal.

(continued on page 8)

(continued from page 7)

9. When the ball goes out of bounds, it shall be thrown into the field of play by the person touching it. He has a right to hold it unmolested for five seconds. In case of a dispute, the umpire shall throw it straight into the field. The thrower-in is allowed five seconds; if he holds it longer it shall go to the opponent. If any side persists in delaying the game the umpire shall call a foul on that side.

10. The umpire shall be the judge of the men and shall note the fouls and notify the referee when three consecutive fouls have been made. He shall have power to disqualify men according to Rule 5.

11. The referee shall be judge of the ball and shall decide when the ball is in play, in bounds, to which side it belongs, and shall keep the time. He shall decide when a goal has been made and keep account of the goals, with any other duties that are usually performed by a referee.

12. The time shall be two fifteen-minute halves, with five minutes rest between.

13. The side making the most goals in that time shall be declared the winner. In the case of a draw the game may, by agreement of the captains, be continued until another goal is made.

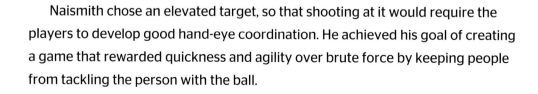

Naismith chose an elevated target, so that shooting at it would require the players to develop good hand-eye coordination. He achieved his goal of creating a game that rewarded quickness and agility over brute force by keeping people from tackling the person with the ball.

Dr. Naismith holds a ball and a peach basket.

On December 21, 1891, the first ever basketball game took place. It ended with a score of 1-0. (Back then, baskets counted for only one point.) Naismith wanted to use a box as the goal, but the custodian could find only a peach basket, which he nailed to the wall. When the basket was scored, the custodian had to use a stepladder to retrieve the ball. Soon, to speed up play, Naismith decided to cut the bottom out of the basket.

Basketball Becomes Popular

Naismith's new game spread quickly. The first game between high school teams was played in 1897, and colleges soon got into the act, too. By the 1930s, several tournaments were being held between the best college teams in the country. Two of these tournaments, the NCAA tournament and the National Invitational Tournament (NIT), are still played today. The NCAA tournament is known as March Madness, because most of the games are played in March, and the students from rival schools provide a loud and raucous audience for the games.

Professional basketball began soon after the invention of the game, but organized leagues took a while to catch on. During the 1920s and 1930s, many independent pro teams went on "barnstorming" tours, playing in different towns against all comers. Attempts were made to start a nationwide professional league, but none really caught on. Finally, the National Basketball Association (NBA) was formed when two pro leagues—the Basketball Association of America and the National Basketball League—merged.

Smith College's class of 1902 women's basketball team poses for a team photograph.

The Trinity College Basketball Team is seen here in 1920-1921.

In 1949-50, the NBA played its first season. For the first few years, the NBA games regularly ended with teams failing to score sixty points. League officials thought of ways to make the game more exciting, so for the 1954–55 season, the NBA introduced the shot clock. This innovation completely altered the way basketball is played. Since then, it has been a part of organized basketball at all levels. The shot clock requires that the team with the ball take a shot within twenty-four seconds (in the NBA) or thirty-five seconds (in college and high school ball). It was because of this rule that offense increased greatly and led to the fast-paced game that is so popular with spectators today.

CHAPTER 2

Players on the Court

Almost any flat surface with enough space to hang a hoop works well for playing basketball. In addition, the game rules can be altered to fit the circumstances. The following two chapters focus on regulation play, the way basketball is played in high school, college, and the NBA.

How it's Played

The objective in basketball is very simple: to score more field goals—the official term for baskets—than the other team. The offense, or team in possession of the ball, tries to take a good shot before the shot clock expires. To do this, the offense runs plays—set series of player movements and passes—to get the ball to a player with an open shot at the basket.

For its part, the defense counters with strategies to prevent the offense from getting a good shot. Individually, defensive players use their bodies and arms to block the offensive player's path to the basket. They may also try to take the ball away from the ball handler (called a steal). As a team, defenses also run their own plays.

A player attempts to score a basket.

For example, an offense player may be double teamed or trapped by a defense player. This involves putting two defenders on the player with the ball to prevent an easy shot.

Where it's Played

The regulation basketball court for the NBA and college levels is a rectangle that is fifty feet wide and ninety-four feet long. Most high school courts are eighty-four feet long. The hoops, or rims, are located at either end of the court. They are ten feet off the ground and attached to backboards that measure six feet across. The backboards are hung so that they are four feet in from the baseline.

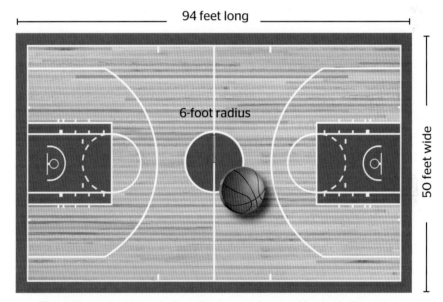

This is the typical layout of a college or professional basketball court.

Several lines are painted on the court. The division line, or midcourt line, separates the backcourt from the frontcourt. After one team makes a basket, the opposing team goes on offense and must bring the ball into the frontcourt within a certain amount of time—eight seconds in the NBA—or they turn the ball over to the other team. A circle with a six-foot radius is painted at the center of the midcourt line. The opening tip-off, or jump ball, takes place within this circle.

The Carrier Dome arena at Syracuse University in New York State is home to the school's basketball team, as well as its football and lacrosse teams. It is the largest domed college stadium in the nation.

Fifteen feet from each backboard lies the foul line (or free-throw line). Each foul line marks the diameter of a circle that is also used for jump balls. A rectangular area underneath each basket is called the foul lane, or lane. Originally, the foul lane was much narrower, and in combination with the circle around the free throw line, it looked like a keyhole. (To this day, the point on the circle farthest from the basket is called the top of the key.) If an offensive player has even one foot in the foul lane, he or she must take a shot within three seconds. The lane and the three-second rule prevent taller, stronger players from setting up close to the basket and taking very easy shots.

The three-point line is an arc that runs from the baseline to behind the top of the key. Shots made from behind this line count for three points instead of two. The NBA three-point line is farther from the basket than the college and high school line.

Player Positions

Only five players from each team are allowed on the court at the same time. Each player has a a special role on the team's defensive and offensive schemes. Typically, teams play with two guards, two forwards, and one center. However, a team may play with three guards, or three forwards, or even two centers. For convenience when designing plays, player positions are often numbered, one through five.

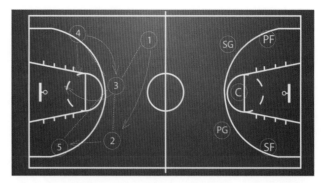

Player positions are seen here on the basketball court.

What's a Guard?

The point guard, or one-guard, is the field general for a basketball team. The point guard runs the offensive plays, so he or she needs to bounce—or dribble—the ball well. Good point guards dribble with their head up, so they know where all the other players are.

Just as important as dribbling is the ability to make good passes. The point guard must deliver the ball accurately, so that teammates can catch the ball and shoot quickly. Accurate passes also prevent the other team from stealing the ball. Passing is so important to the game that if a pass leads directly to a score, the player who made the pass gets an assist. A high number of assists in a game indicates that the point guard is doing a good job.

The point guard is often the first line of defense, as he or she will usually guard the other team's primary ball handler. On defense, the point guard tries to anticipate the other team's plays, stealing the ball when the opportunity presents itself.

Point guards are often the shortest players on the team. This increases their ball control, because they are closer to the ground and don't have to bounce the ball as high.

Michael Jordan of the Chicago Bulls prepares to dunk.
He played shooting guard through his career.

The team's guard, sometimes called the two guard or shooting guard, usually scores a lot of baskets. Usually, this means he or she is an accurate outside shooter. However, some two-guards are only mediocre shooters who score by penetrating, or getting close to the basket using their speed and ball-handling skills.

The best two-guards can move in any direction, releasing shots from any spot on the court. Michael Jordan, who was a two-guard, became one of the game's top scorers because he was both a great shooter and a great ball handler. He was also very creative and original with his moves.

Two-guards are usually bigger than point guards, but they tend to be smaller than the forwards or centers, so they aren't expected to rebound much.

What's a Forward?

Guards play away from the basket, but forwards play close to the basket, often just under it. They are generally taller and bigger than guards. At higher levels of play, forwards are categorized as small forwards or power forwards. Small forwards, who play what is called the three position, are expected to score. Power forwards, who play in the four position, are expected to rebound and play tough defense.

Forwards are not expected to be as good as guards at handling the ball. Besides, they don't need to have great outside shots because they play closer to the basket.

Tim Duncan is one of the most famous forwards of all times.

What's a Center?

The team's center plays in the middle of the team's offense and defense, at the five position. Centers are generally the biggest and tallest players on the court. They must provide strong defense against the other team's biggest player, while also preventing opposing guards and forwards from penetrating for easy shots. Good centers can block opponents' shots, and they are good rebounders, too.

It is not crucial for the center to be a good offensive player, but the better teams often have a center who can score. Because of their position, centers usually take most of their shots standing close to the basket.

The pro game has been long dominated by great centers such as Wilt Chamberlain, Bill Russell, Kareem Abdul-Jabbar, and Shaquille O'Neal.

Wilt Chamberlain

Bill Russell

Kareem Abdul-Jabbar

Shaquille O'Neal

Bill Russell defends against Wilt Chamberlain, who has the ball.

"Stick the J": Basketball Lingo

Basketball players, just like athletes in other sports, have their own specialized words or lingo. If you want to sound like a "gym rat" use some of these expressions:

game: Good basketball skills, as in, "she's got game."

boards: The backboards. Also, rebounds: "He had ten boards in that game."

stick the J: Make a jump shot. "You can dribble, but can you stick the J?"

alley-oop: A pass thrown high in the air above the basket so that another player can slam dunk it.

gym rat: A player who is always practicing basketball, often alone. Real gym rats are the first ones to arrive at practice and the last ones to leave.

stuff: To dunk the ball. Also, to block a shot: "He got stuffed while attempting a layup".

A player slam dunks the basketball.

zebras: At most levels, the referees wear black and white striped shirts.

we've got next: In playground basketball, the team that wins gets to stay on the court. If you want to play the winners, say, "We've got next," to stake your claim.

run: To play basketball. On the playground, people might ask you if you "want to run" with them, meaning play basketball with them.

This is a typical referee uniform.

Role of the Coach

The responsibilities of the head coach include creating the lineups, calling the plays on both offense and defense, and handling the substitutions during the game. A good coach is also a teacher who constantly uses his or her experience to help players improve their game.

During the game, a coach will tell the team which plays to run by using hand signals or code numbers. For offensive plays, coaches always try to take advantage of any weakness in the other team's defense. This could be a mismatch such as a short player guarding a tall one or a slow player guarding a quick one. A coach decides when to call for a timeout. This brief period of rest is essential for players.

Red Auerbach, one of the most prominent coaches of all time, coached the Washington Capitals, the Tri-Cities Blackhawks, and the Boston Celtics.

CHAPTER 3

The Game

Since the game was first played, many additions have been made to the rules of basketball. But the general principles of the game have remained unchanged. As in Naismith's day, the objective of the game is still to put the ball in the basket.

Penn State's Andrew Jones (left) faces off with Purdue's JaJuan Johnson during a jump ball.

Starting the Game

There are four quarters of play in a basketball game. In the NBA, each quarter is twelve minutes long. Depending on the league, college and high school games are made up of two twenty-minute halves or four ten-minute quarters. If the game is tied at the end of regulation time, a five-minute overtime period is played.

The first quarter begins with a tip-off, or jump ball. Two players, one from each team, stand at midcourt with the other players gathered around them. When the referee throws the ball high in the air, the two players try to knock it to a teammate. Referees may also call for a jump ball at other times during the game, as when they are unable to determine which team knocked the ball out of bounds.

In college and high school, officials use the alternate-possession rule after the opening tip-off. This means that the team that does not take possession of the opening tip will be awarded possession of the ball if there is a held ball (two players from different teams each have possession) or at the beginning of the next quarter. For the rest of the game, possession alternates.

Illegally charging into a defender is a foul.

What's a Foul?

A foul is when a player, accidentally or deliberately, breaks a rule. The most common type of foul occurs when a defensive player makes illegal contact with an opponent who is trying to shoot. After some defensive fouls, a shooter is awarded an uncontested shot (or "free" throw) from behind this free throw line. Each free throw that is made counts as one point.

Offensive players commit fouls, too. They sometimes illegally charge into a defender or unfairly prevent a defender from getting into position. In most cases, offensive fouls do not result in free throws.

In the NBA game, a player is disqualified after committing five fouls, whether offensive or defensive. In lower-level games, players are disqualified after committing a sixth foul. A disqualified player may be replaced by another player, but he or she is not allowed to re-enter the game.

Some Common Fouls

charging: An offensive foul called when a player runs into a defender who has established position.

elbowing: Making contact with your elbows in an attempt to move or push away the other player.

flagrant foul: Called for excessive or unnecessary contact.

holding: Grabbing or otherwise preventing a player from moving freely.

loose ball foul: A foul that occurs when neither team has possession, such as during a rebound.

over-the-back: A foul that occurs when a player makes contact while reaching over from behind a player in position to rebound.

(continued on page 26)

(continued from page 25)

reaching in: Making contact with the ball handler when trying to go for a steal.

technical foul: Any action the referee believes is detrimental to the game. Technical fouls can be given to anybody on the team, not just the players on the court; even coaches can get technical fouls. A technical foul results in the other team getting one free throw.

It is against the rules to prevent another player from moving freely. The player in white is clearly fouling the other player.

How the Ball Is Handled

In Naismith's original vision of the game, a player had to pass the ball right away. But the game developed two rules to allow players to move with the ball: the pivot and the dribble.

A player with the ball may pivot, or turn on one foot, in any direction without having to pass the ball. Once a player establishes a pivot foot, he or she cannot then pivot on the other foot. If he or she then switches pivots, it constitutes a violation called traveling, which leads to a turnover, meaning the possession is given to the other team.

This is the 1899 Kansas University team, with the coach, Dr. Naismith.

Pivoting

An important part of every player's moves, especially centers, are called pivots. When you post up, or play with your back to the hoop, a good pivot move will allow you to move toward the basket and use your height to get off a good shot. Posting up requires you to use size and strength to force your defender out of position.

An important component in a good post move is the ability to fake. For this, you pretend to take a shot to get the defender to change position. Then, you pivot and spin to change the direction of the play. This creates distance between you and the defender, allowing an easier shot.

Keep your head up and eyes forward when pivoting.

A player is allowed to take one step with the ball. If you want to take more than one step with the ball, you must dribble it, or bounce it on the floor. Because you are not actually carrying the ball, moving while dribbling is not a traveling violation. You can use either hand to dribble, and even switch hands, but you cannot use both hands at the same time. This violation is called double dribbling, and is also a turnover.

Shooting a Basket

Many different types of shots can be used to put the ball in the hoop. The most common shots are jump shots and layups. A player takes a jump shot, or jumper, by leaping in the air and releasing the shot at the highest point. Just about all outside shots are jump shots. Jump shots are effective because they can be released quickly, and when they are taken while running, they are very hard to block.

A layup, on the other hand, is a shot taken very close to the hoop. A layup is generally much easier to make than a jump shot.

Layups

To make a layup easier, use the backboard. Dribble the ball until you are about five feet from the basket. (You can dribble even closer when you are first learning this shot.) Pick up the ball in one hand and then take a step toward the basket. If you are shooting with your right hand, jump off your left foot. Aim your shot at the box behind the rim and try to bank the ball into the hoop. You should keep practicing until you can make a layup each time you shoot.

A player attempts to perfect his layup.

A shot in which the ball is thrown straight down through the hoop is called a slam dunk or a jam. To make this shot, the player must be able to jump high in the air. Obviously, taller players have an advantage in making this shot.

A very effective shot that has fallen out of favor is the hook shot. For a hook shot, you turn to the side, extend your shooting arm high in the air, and release the ball one-handed. Kareem Abdul-Jabbar used his hook shot, nicknamed the sky hook, to score more points than any other player in NBA history.

Running Plays

Individual ball-handling skills and a good shooting touch are great to have, but basketball games are won and lost as a team. On offense, all five players must be involved to create good scoring chances. And on defense, all five players must work hard to help one another out and make it difficult for the other team to score.

Basketball is all about team effort.

Offensive Plays

Next time you watch a good team play offense, look at the action away from the ball. You will see that each player knows his or her role in the offense. There are hundreds of different offensive plays that teams will run, many of which involve all five players. But there are some very effective plays that require only two players. These include the pick and the give-and-go.

To set a pick, also called a screen, you stand still beside the opponent who is defending your teammate with the ball. Your teammate then dribbles so that he or she runs the defender into you. This often creates enough space for your teammate to attempt an uncontested shot. In a variation called the pick-and-roll, you set a pick and then turn ("roll") toward the basket. Turn quickly and use your backside to pin the defender you picked. Then when your teammate passes the ball back to you, you'll often have an open shot at the basket.

Defensive players try to steal the ballfrom an offensive player or prevent him from having clear passing and shooting lanes.

For a give-and-go, you simply pass the ball to a teammate ("give") and quickly break toward the basket ("go"). If your defender reacts slowly, your teammate can quickly bounce-pass the ball back to you, and you'll have an open path to the basket.

Other offensive plays include the fast break, also called the running game, the high-post and low-post, the triangle, and motion offense. Different offensive tactics are used depending on the defense's strengths and weaknesses.

Defensive Plays

Although it is critical to score points, a good defense is just as important as a good offense. Like offense, defense in basketball is a team concept that starts with strong individual skills.

To make a steal without fouling, a good individual defender anticipates the play and then knocks the ball away without making contact with the ball handler. The defender may also make a steal by anticipating a pass. It is usually much easier to steal a pass than to take the ball from another player, so being able to see the entire floor and understand the other team's offense is a critical skill.

Shot blocking is another crucial defensive skill. This is an important part of a center's game. If a shot is on the way up, it is legal to knock it away. However, once the ball reaches the top of its arc, no player can touch it. Interfering with a ball in its downward flight is a violation called goaltending. This goaltending rule prevents tall players from standing in front of the basket and blocking every shot.

Basketball has become an international sport. Here, Elton Brown, of Brose Baskets Bamberg, defends as Aubrey Reese, of Skyliners, takes a shot during a playoff game in Frankfurt, Germany.

How to Play Defense

When defending, it is important to keep your body relaxed. Bend at the knees and keep your weight forward. Keep your back straight and lean into a crouch, holding your head up straight. As the saying goes, "you play defense with your feet." If you are up on the balls of your feet, you can change directions quickly. But you have to use your hands, too. Keep your arms out away from your body and move your hands to block the passing lanes. Try to swipe the ball from below to avoid a foul.

When playing defense, be sure to look left and right to see if an opponent is moving in to set a pick. Don't focus too closely on the ball. Good ball handlers can easily beat you with a crossover dribble or a ball fake. Instead, try to focus on your opponent's waist. By watching the waist, you will not be fooled by the fakes a good player will try to use, because the waist has to move in the same direction as the player is going.

The defender tries to block the ball handler.

Team defenses have their own set ups, just like offenses. The most common is man-to-man defense, in which each defender guards one offensive player. In colleges and high school, your team might also use a zone defense, in which you guard an area of the court instead of a specific player. If a ball handler comes into your area, you play aggressive defense against him or her.

Defenders team up to prevent the offense from taking a shot.

Defenses may also try a half-court or full-court press, strategies that keep the offense from getting the ball up-court easily. Some presses call for defenders to trap, meaning they force the ball handler to the sideline and then double-team him or her, forcing a turnover. Presses often confuse the offense and force turnovers from violations or errant passes. The best way to beat a full-court press is to run a fast break, with quick, accurate passing. The ball then gets into the frontcourt before the defense can get in position to trap.

Temple University Owls men's basketball player Lavoy Allen goes up to grab a rebound during a game against Duquesne University.

Getting a Rebound

One of the keys to winning is rebounding, or getting possession of the ball after a missed shot. Good rebounders don't mind getting under the basket and playing a little rough, if necessary. Height and strength are obviously advantages in being a good rebounder, but proper positioning is just as important.

On defense, getting good position is called boxing out. When a shot is taken, you should establish position between the basket and the player you are guarding. Then turn, so that you are facing the basket. It's important to maintain contact with the player you are boxing out, so remember to put your "butt in the gut" of your opponent. Keep your elbows out and hands up. Watch the flight of the ball, anticipating where it will bounce if it doesn't go in the hoop. If the shot rattles off the rim, explode toward the ball and grab it with both hands.

Offensive players try to rebound, too. Getting an offensive rebound is crucial, since it gives your team another chance to score.

John Wooden, the most successful NCAA coach ever, once said, "It's what we learn after we know it all that really counts." Even though you may have already known everything covered here, it is a safe bet that there is still a lot more for you to learn.

John Wooden , UCLA head coach, is seen here on campus, 1960.

CHAPTER 4

Getting Involved

Basketball can be played almost anywhere.

Where can you go to play a good game of basketball? Luckily, there are many ways in which you can play, whether as part of your school team, with other groups, or on your own.

There are many programs in most middle schools for both boys and girls that allow you to play in organized games against other schools. There are basketball teams in most high schools too.

Tryouts can be very competitive in bigger schools and not everyone makes the team. But if you just want to play for fun, you can see if your school offers intramural games. These are games between students who want to play without the structure and extensive practice the varsity teams require. Intramural teams typically have players of all skill levels.

Outside of school, in many communities, you can sign up for leagues at the YMCA and YWCA, or other youth organizations. These leagues often are broken down by age or skill level.

You could also attend one of the many basketball camps that are held around the country, usually during the summer. At camp, you'll live, eat, and breathe basketball for a week or two. These are great places to meet other players and learn good techniques from experienced coaches.

Preparing Right

You must always make sure you have the right protective equipment, regardless of when or where you play. Boys should always wear an athletic supporter. Knee pads or elbow pads are also a good idea, especially if you are playing on an outdoor court. It is also a good idea to wear a mouthpiece and sports goggles, if you wear glasses.

Warming up before you begin playing is very important.

It is important to stretch major muscles when preparing for a game. Always stretch before and after playing to prevent cramps. Prior to stretching, warm up a little with a short jog. (Warm muscles are easier to stretch.) Start your stretches with the muscles in your lower back and legs. These are the biggest muscles in your body and the ones that get the hardest workout while playing. Stand with your legs apart and toes pointed outward. Then bend slowly and steadily several times over both knees and straight ahead.

To stretch your hamstrings, sit on the floor with your knees together and your legs straight, and try to touch your toes.

Groin pulls can take a long time to heal, so stretch your groin muscles as well. For this, sit on the floor and bring your feet together, sole to sole. Then try touching your knees to the ground, gently pushing with your elbows to get a better stretch.

After stretching, do a more vigorous warm up to get your body ready for the real action. Warm-ups do not have to be complicated—just jog around the gym, and then dribble the ball for several minutes. Use this time to get a sense of how your body is feeling. Before a team

Juan Carlos Navarro warms up before a Euroleague basketball game.

practice, your coach will probably run a series of drills, including wind sprints (running very quickly from one end of the gym to another) and shooting and rebounding drills.

To play your best, you need to be in good physical condition. This means exercising regularly, in addition to just playing the game. An excellent way of building up stamina and getting your legs in shape is to go running or jogging.

Doing push-ups regularly helps build upper body strength.

You can shoot and rebound more effectively by doing push-ups and pull-ups to build your upper body strength. Light weight lifting may also help.

Basketball Variations

If you don't have enough players for a full game of basketball, you might try HORSE or Around the World. In HORSE, you take a shot from anywhere on the court. If you make it, the other players have to make the same exact shot. If the other player fails to make the shot, he or she gets a letter: H-O-R-S and then E. Once you have HORSE, you are out of the game. The winner is the last player without HORSE.

In Around the World, each player has to make shots in order, from specific places on the court. You can't move on to the next shot until you make the one you are taking. Play usually starts with a layup from the right side, followed by shots from around the court, and ending with a layup from the left side. The winner is the first player to go "Around the World."

Playing Better: Skills and Drills

You can practice shooting by playing games like Around the World. To develop your ball-handling skills, dribble, dribble, and then dribble some more. Keep the ball low at all times, and remember to work on both hands.

To become a better passer, you don't even need another player. Tape three targets at different heights on a wall, and then try to hit them with chest passes and bounce passes. Once you can hit each one consistently, move back until you can hit the targets from twenty feet away or farther.

Don't overlook your defensive skills. You can improve your defensive quickness and stamina by slide-stepping from one end of the court to the other and back. For this, stand in the proper defensive position, and then move sideways, quickly sliding your feet without crossing your legs. If you are doing it correctly, you'll feel a good burn in your upper legs.

If you already play basketball, you know that it is a fun sport that's also good for your health. If you have never played, consider basketball as a great way to develop your physical skills and build friendships that can last your entire life. If you are wondering why basketball is so popular all around the world, hit the court and find out!

Glossary

barnstorm To tour through rural districts, putting on exhibitions.

confined Restricted or held within a location.

detrimental Harmful or damaging.

double-team To guard a single player with two defenders.

dribble To bounce the basketball.

errant Straying out of bounds.

fast break An attempt to score quickly by running up the court before the other team can get into defensive position.

field goal A basket, or goal, made when the ball is in play.

jump shot A shot taken by jumping in the air and releasing the ball at the top of the leap.

lane The painted rectangle under the basket at either end of the court.

penetrate To drive past a defender and get near the basket with the ball.

raucous Boisterous and disorderly.

shrouded Hidden or concealed.

stamina Endurance or staying power.

traveling Taking more than one step with the ball without dribbling; a basketball violation that results in a turnover.

turnover Giving the other team possession of the ball.

vigorous Active or energetic.

For More Information

Amateur Athletic Union (AAU)
320 Quail Run South
Altus, OK 73521
Web site: http://www.aausports.org

National Basketball Association (NBA)
League Office
645 Fifth Avenue, 19th Floor
New York, NY 10022
Web site: http://www.nba.com

National Association of Police Athletic/Activities Leagues, Inc.
658 West Indiantown Road, Suite 201
Jupiter, FL 33458
(561) 745-5535
Web site: http://www.nationalpal.org

The National Collegiate Athletic Association
700 W. Washington Street
P.O. Box 6222
Indianapolis, Indiana 46206-6222
(317) 917 6222
Web site: http://www.ncaa.org

USA Basketball
5465 Mark Dabling Boulevard
Colorado Springs, CO 80918-3842
(719) 590 4800
Web site: http://www.usab.com

YMCA of the USA
101 North Wacker Drive
Chicago, IL 60606
(800) 872 9622
Web site: http://www.ymca.net

YWCA of the USA
1015 18th Street
NW, Suite 1100
Washington, DC 20036
(202) 467 0801
Web site: http://www.ywca.org

Web Sites

Due to the changing nature of Internet links, Rosen Publishing has developed an online list of Web sites related to the subject of this book. This site is updated regularly. Please use this link to access the list:

http://www.rosenlinks.com/STTS/Bask

For Further Reading

Bird, Larry, and Earvin Magic Johnson. *When the Game Was Ours*. New York, NY: Brilliance Audio on MP3-CD, 2011.

DeVenzio, Dick. *Stuff Good Players Should Know: Intelligent Basketball from A to Z*. Austin, TX: PGC Basketball, 2011.

Editors of Sports Illustrated. *Sports Illustrated: The Basketball Book*. New York, NY: Sports Illustrated, 2007.

Grange, Michael, and Wayne Embry. *Basketball's Greatest Stars*. Richmond Hill, ON: Firefly books, 2013.

Halberstam, David. *The Breaks of the Game*. New York, NY: Hyperion, 2009.

Herren, Chris, and Bill Reynolds. *Basketball Junkie: A Memoir*. New York, NY: St. Martin's Griffin, 2012.

Jackson, Phil, and Hugh Delehanty. *Eleven Rings: The Soul of Success*. New York, NY: Penguin Press HC, 2013.

Krause, Jerry, Don Meyer, and Jerry Meyer. *Basketball Skills & Drills*. Champaign, IL: Human Kinetics, 2007.

Lupica, Mike. *True Legend*. New York, NY: Puffin, 2013.

Phelps, Richard. *Basketball For Dummies*. Hoboken, NJ: For Dummies, 2011.

Simmons, Bill, and Malcolm Gladwell. *The Book of Basketball: The NBA According to The Sports Guy*. New York, NY: ESPN Books, 2010.

Bibliography

Garfinkle, Howard. *Five-Star Basketball Drills*. New York, NY: McGraw-Hill, 1998.

Krause, Jerry. *Coaching Basketball*. New York, NY: McGraw-Hill, 2002.

NBA.com. "Official Rules of the National Basketball Association." Retrieved May 1, 2006 (http://www.nba.com/analysis/rules_index.html).

Wolff, Alexander. *100 Years of Hoops: A Fond Look Back at the Sport of Basketball*. New York, NY: Warner Books, 1997.

Wooden, John, and Steve Jamison. *Wooden on Leadership*. New York, NY: McGraw-Hill, 2005.

Index

About the Authors

Forest G. Campbell is a writer who lives in Westchester County, New York. An avid sportsman, he has played basketball, softball, and volleyball for many years on various youth and adult teams.

Fred Ramen is a writer who lives in New York City. A longtime sports fan, he has previously written about basketball in his biography of one of the game's all-time greats, Jerry West.

Photo Credits

The photographs in this book are used by permission and through the courtesy of: Cover photo by © Flashon Studio/shutterstock.com; © broeb/shutterstock.com, 1, 3, 6, 8, 25; © Carlos Delgado/commons.wikimedia.org, 4; © Canicula/shutterstock.com, 4; © D. Gordon E. Robertson/commons.wikimedia.org, 5; © Aspen Photo/shutterstock.com, 7, 34; © http://www.bkprostejov.cz/foto.php?img=http://www.bkprostejov.cz/galerie/C_1172178795.jpg/commons.wikimedia.org, 9; © unknown/commons.wikimedia.org, 10; © Duke University Archives/commons.wikimedia.org, 11; © dotshock/shutterstock.com, 12, 20, 28; © Kittichai/shutterstock.com, 13; © Darry2385/commons.wikimedia.org, 14; © My Life Graphic/shutterstock.com, 15; © Steve Lipofsky/commons.wikimedia.org, 16; © Author Keith Allison/commons.wikimedia.org, 17, 18; © Cpl. Lameen Witter/commons.wikimedia.org, 18; © Fred Palumbo, World Telegram staff photographer/commons.wikimedia.org, 18; © Sporting News via Getty Images/gettyimages.in, 18; Wickedgood/dreamstime.com, 18; © flickr user cgilmour/commons.wikimedia.org, 19; © JaimieDuplass/shutterstock.com, 21; © Steve Lipofsky Basketballphoto.com/commons.wikimedia.org, 21; © Richard Paul Kane/shutterstock.com, 22, 23, 33; © PavelShchegolev/shutterstock.com, 24 © eileenmeyer/shutterstock.com, 26; © Clendening History of Medicine Library, University of Kansas Medical Center/shutterstock.com, 26; © bikeriderlondon/shutterstock.com, 27; © FL Smith/commons.wikimedia.org, 29; © muzsy/shutterstock.com, 27; Fingerhut/shutterstock.com, 31; © ARENA Creative/shutterstock.com, 32; © Associated Students, University of California, Los Angeles/commons.wikimedia.org, 35; © George Muresan/shutterstock.com, 36, 37; © Sergey Dubrov/shutterstock.com, 38; © Andresr/shutterstock.com, 38; © Natursports/commons.wikimedia.org, 39; © michaeljung/shutterstock.com, 40; © Visionsi/shutterstock.com, 40.